Humor, Humility, Homelessness

Life in a Small Town's Shelter

———●◆►◄◆●———

by Arthur P. Palmer

Cover Art & Final Page Illustrations
by Milton Reyman

Interior Illustrations by Arkettype

Humor, Humility, Homelessness
Life in a Small Town's Shelter

by Arthur P. Palmer

published by

ARKETT PUBLISHING
division of Arkettype
PO Box 36, Gaylordsville, CT 06755
860-350-4007 • Fax 860-355-3970
www.local-author.com

ISBN 978-1-0880-5120-7

Printed in USA

Humor, Humility, Homelessness
Life in a Small Town's Shelter

by Arthur P. Palmer

———◆•▸◦◂•◆———

Table of Contents

Dedication 5

Acknowledgment 7

Foreword 9

Disclaimer 11

Introduction 13

Chapter 1: No Place To Hide 17

Chapter 2: The Hole 25

Chapter 3: Shadows 31

Chapter 4: Your God 39

Chapter 5: Spitting Out The Poison 49

Chapter 6: Ghosts. 57

Chapter 7: Empty Places 65

Chapter 8: Saints & Sinners. 71

Chapter 9: This Is Not All 79

Chapter 10: I Was Born For This. 85

Epilogue: Sandbox 91

Final Notes To Friends 95

For More Information on How You Can Help 97

———◆•▸◦◂•◆———

Arthur P. Palmer

Dedication

This book needs to be dedicated to many people. The most important is my wife Ellen who, for the first five years of my being a shelter coordinator, worked side-by-side with me, slowing my anger when things were getting out of control early on. When we first met, she saw something good inside me before I knew it existed. She stayed by my side during the hard times of addiction and alcohol abuse: times that were sometimes so bad that I would have left myself, if I could have escaped my body. I lived long enough to write this book because of her.

My two children Travus and Chelsea helped me ground myself, and gave me more reason to change. My younger sisters Judy and Lisa, and my brother Jay, who have always been my family and are now also my friends. My mom, Jane, who taught me kindness when I could not see much in the world around me. She set the blocks in my foundation.

To the wonderful people I have worked with for the past 15 years at the homeless shelter. Especially all the coordinators who taught me needed lessons, who made it a safe place to be, a safe place to sleep, a nightly home for those who did not have one.

To Arthur Hopkins and Dan Robles, my first shelter teachers.

To the memory of my good friend, Oscar Rasmussen, who always saw the good in everyone.

To Peg Molina, who got me involved in one of the most important journeys in my life.

To Jack Gilpin, a man who ministers to all no matter their religion or spirituality.

To Justin Cullmer, a young man who taught this old man that much can be accomplished by only a few who are driven and have connections.

To all my close friends and family (including my homeless family) for all the support in times of need. My heart to your heart!

To Loaves and Fishes for feeding many with open hearts and hands.

Michelle Obama is quoted as saying "Find people who make you better!" All of you have done that for me.

To all those working in any of the social services with small budgets and not enough staff: thank you.

To the sea of homeless, the poor, the mentally ill; especially those who have lost all hope: hold on! We will keep swimming toward you. Don't give up: don't ever give up.

———◆◆×◆◆———

Acknowledgments

Cover concept and final page art by Milton Reyman.
Editing by Ellen and Chelsea Palmer.
Transcribing by Chelsea Palmer.
Audiobook by Travus Palmer and Jessica Block.

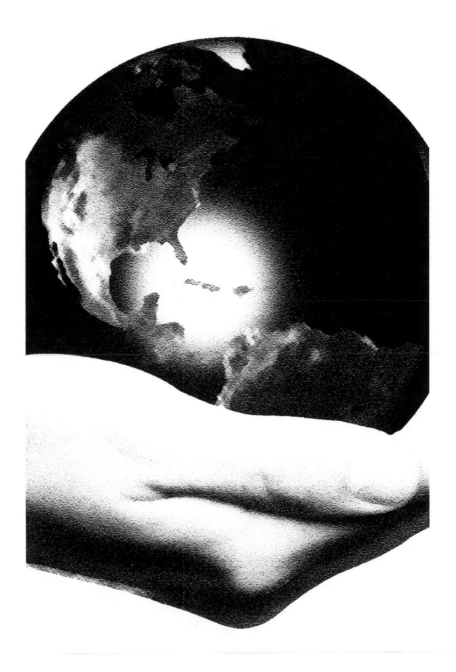

Foreword

The second Great Commandment, in both Christianity and Judaism, is, "You shall love your neighbor as yourself." (To clarify, "your neighbor" means any and every human.) Most of us understand that commandment as a kind of parallel to the Golden Rule ("Do unto others as you would have them do unto you.")

But what if, instead, "Love your neighbor as yourself" meant loving your neighbor as if that were you? As if what was happening to your neighbor were happening to you too? Think about how different the world would be if everyone lived according to that understanding of the commandment.

I can honestly say that I have seen a good practical demonstration of that kind of behavior in the work of Arthur Palmer and his colleagues in the New Milford Homeless Shelter Coalition. For eight years I was the priest at St. John's Episcopal Church in New Milford, Connecticut, one of the churches that provided space for the Coalition and its guests, and I was privileged to witness how Art, his fellow coordinators, and their volunteers ministered (which is what they were doing) to people whom the overwhelming majority of society either ignores or wants forcibly removed from their field of vision.

In this wonderful book, you will meet some of those people. You will hear their stories, and you will come to know that they are your neighbors. You will also hear something of Art's own story, which is intensely personal, but speaks truths about life on this earth that are universal, and timeless. And you will see, in particular, Art's experience of a truth to which all the major religions point: that in service to others—especially to the most deprived, the most deeply wounded, the most often shoved aside – lies the most profound fulfillment of what it means to be a human. Thanks for writing this book, Art.

—Rev. Jack Gilpin

Disclaimer

The views inside this book and any comments I make are completely my own. I have no training in psychiatry or psychology besides the few classes I have taken to enhance my understanding while working at the shelter. All that I have written are personal views I have put down on paper while working on the front lines of the fight to end homelessness. If you see things here you don't agree with, you will have to write your own book. This is how I have seen the world and felt things along my own path.

I also read a lot, if I have put something in my words that has been previously published by someone else, I truly apologize! Some people look at this as a theft. I look at it as an admiration for someone else's wonderful ideas that are close to my own, but with the inability to remember who they are or where I read them. I applaud all of those who work on or write about our homeless problems. We have a monumental task before us.

Before you start reading this book, there is something that I recently read by author Ryan Holiday. Please keep this in mind while reading stories about our homeless shelter. Thanks.

Ryan Holiday said, "I was reading a book recently and I could feel a part of my mind trying to find a way to blame the subjects of the book for their problems. The reason for doing this, I came to reflect, was that if it was their fault, then I wouldn't really have to care. I wouldn't have to do anything or change any of my beliefs. I think it is this impulse that explains so much of where we are in the world today."

Introduction

Many years ago, I joined a group of people who had established a winter freeze shelter. This is basically a homeless shelter open just during winter months to keep the homeless population alive. We are in New England, where winter temperatures can drop to -20 or even -30 degrees Fahrenheit. This is the most important volunteer work I have ever done, and definitely the most rewarding. While sometimes it's been a rollercoaster of events and feelings, it's always worth it!

Every position we have is completely volunteer-based: board members, coordinators, overnight volunteers, laundering bedding, scheduling and paperwork. No one gets paid and we do not receive any money towards this cause from our town, the state or the federal government. Any funding we receive is from personal donors and from fundraising events. Most of all, there would be no shelter without the churches. Area churches in the center of town give us a space each month to house the homeless.

We appreciate this immensely, but not nearly as much as the homeless who use it. We need to remember that these people are no different than we are. Some are fighting inner demons, some are fighting wars past, some are just fighting for survival. We should never turn our backs on them.

<hr />

I started writing this years ago, not so much as a book, more like a journal of my experiences. I wrote on nights I stayed as an overnight volunteer and continued when I became one of the coordinators who would check the guests in each night. Intoxication from alcohol or drugs, violence, or a bad demeanor towards fellow shelter attendees were reasons to hand out a sleeping bag and send them away. This responsibility is never taken lightly as all of the coordinators know that the safety of all the people inside depended on how well we did our jobs. If the weather is dangerously cold, the coordinator can decide to stay overnight along with the overnight volunteers and allow the intoxicated guest to stay. Should violent behavior escalate at any point during the night or the guest refuses to leave the premises, the police are called.

There are consequences to all our actions in this life, and we had to be there to remind some people of that. Name any emotion and at one point or another you will find it inside a shelter. After reading parts of my journal and sharing it with my wife Ellen, I decided to share these stories with everyone to help humanize the homeless to people who had never been around them and share the incredible amounts of humor, humility and compassion that I have been fortunate enough to have witnessed.

———◆◆◆◆———

When I started working in the shelter I did not expect to find much humor there. Surprisingly, it permeates the place: I found it everywhere. It is part of survival, part of moving from one day to the next, especially if the next day does not look like it is going to be any better. This does not seem to make sense in the beginning but as time goes by it becomes very understandable. It warms the heart and soul. I am writing this book because of it!

The shelter has changed my life, the way I live it, and the way I look at the world. The way I look at people who do not understand the short distance between having a wonderful life and being stranded in a world of shadows and contempt. If we can't find the justice we look for, we have to provide it ourselves or all is lost.

———◆◆◆◆———

While reading this book, you will eventually come across some stories that are not about homelessness. I wrote in my journal every night that I stayed there. If it was late and I could not sleep, I wrote. So you will see some ravings of a sleepless madman from time to time. What was written in this journal, stayed in the journal!

Each chapter will start with a poem that was also written at the shelter. These were not put in order, they were picked at random.

14

Some are very dark. I have found that writing down things of darkness gets them out of my system, at least for a while.

I told you in the beginning that I have some great stories and experiences, so it's about time that I stop babbling and tell you about some of my friends who stayed at the shelter. We refer to them as our guests, and no names were used, as every human being deserves their privacy.

———◆▸✕◂◆———

Arthur P. Palmer

CHAPTER 1

No Place To Hide

I watch the damaged people
All lined up in a row
Afraid of all life's mystery
Afraid of all the things they know
Some just never grew up
A beaten child, adulthood stunted
Always wander that same hallway
The smell of fear, where fathers hunted
Others shy, with heads bowed low
Afraid to talk, they never smile
Someone told them they were worthless
And they've believed it all this while
Every crowd becomes a battle
Waged on them till setting sun
Every day too long to live through
No place to hide, nowhere to run

Our guest was small in stature but larger-than-life in person. I knew him back in school and he was "quite a character"—that was before anyone even knew he was bipolar. As tough as things might go for him, he was always in a good mood.

One night in a talkative mood, he kept on chatting after lights out. I told him to quiet down because others needed to sleep. Ten minutes later, he told the guy next to him that he had broken his arm twice in his life. Someone in the back yelled "Three times if you don't shut up!" We all laughed for awhile and soon, it was quiet for all.

The same guest had a joke for everything. I never had any problems with him. He was non-violent and very funny. A few years after this story, he found housing, but was ordered to take medicine daily. Within a few months he was forgetting things and acting like a zombie. I knew he needed a place to live but I really miss who he used to be.

I have met people who have problems separating stories in the newspaper from one another. An older guest of ours asked if I had seen the newspaper yet. When I told him that I had not, he told me that the police went up to the space shuttle and arrested a man for hitting his wife. He was very serious about the whole thing so I thanked him for telling me about it!

I'm not the kind of person who is easily intimidated, yet the first time I met this guest I had to back up to see the top of his head. He was a very large African American gentleman about 6'2", probably weighing in at about 280 lbs. He was a gentle giant, luckily, who was funny when he wasn't trying to be. He could also giggle like a child, which was catching if you were around him when he started.

One night one of the other coordinators saw him wearing a new hat and complimented him on how good it looked, saying "Nice hat, where did you get it?" With a mischievous look he replied "Your house!" That was the strange sense of humor we got used to being around him. His hobby at the shelter was taking apart radios to make them work better. Many of us would pick up radios from thrift stores so he would have a project. As far as I know, he never got one back together again!

I am lucky enough to own a beautiful old motorcycle that I've been known to ride in the middle of winter here on the East Coast, as long as the roads are dry and the temperatures are bearable. On one of these rides in December of 2007, I saw a male guest standing at a bus stop, shaving his bald head with a pink disposable razor. I honked my horn and waved at him as I went by.

Later that week at the shelter I asked him if he had seen some crazy guy ride by on a motorcycle. He told me he had seen one at the bus stop. I told him it was me to which he replied "You all look the same to me!" I said "Motorcycle riders, or old white guys?" He said "Yeah!" One answer, one word, discussion over!

———◆◆◆◆———

My next story is humorous and sad, all rolled into one. People in our shelter care for one another and always give coordinators a heads up when something is going wrong. One night, someone told me that a guest was standing over the sink and that there was blood in it. When I went in to check, I found that unfortunately, it was true. I called another coordinator to help me take him to the hospital. He did not want to go, even as sick as he was.

He told us that three years ago, in another town, he had fallen and hurt one of his knees pretty badly. After taking care of his knee, he said the hospital put him on a floor with all the crazy people. I told him we were his friends and wouldn't let that happen. We were inside one of the treatment rooms waiting for a doctor when he said he knew what his problem was. When we asked him what was wrong, this is the story we were told:

"A long, long time ago, there was a poison on the earth that killed all the dinosaurs. Now, there are some people out there who know where that poison is, and they don't like homeless people, so they dig it up and put it in pipe tobacco because homeless people can't afford cigarettes so they roll pipe tobacco in papers and smoke that." He told us that if the doctors couldn't fix him "I'm gonna go extinct!"

I had to leave in a hurry so I didn't laugh in his face. The other guy wasn't so lucky so he just put his head down and covered his mouth. I explained to the doctor in the hall that whatever he found wrong, any medicine he had to prescribe would be to counteract the dinosaur poison or seriously, he would not take it.

Sometimes, you really have to go to someone else's world to communicate: there's simply no other way around it. Sadly, our friend had a rare blood disease that was very hard to treat. Our guest became extinct about two years after that episode. I miss hearing his stories and I occasionally miss visiting him in his world. Rest in peace, my friend.

———◆◆◆◆———

There are fewer women in the shelter than men, and I'm okay with those statistics. It's hard enough being on the streets without having to worry about the extra abuse people can inflict on you. Many of the women I've met stay better groomed than most of the men, and want with all their heart to be anywhere else than where they have ended up. Occasionally, though, we have a woman who can out-party our most famous party animals at the shelter.

A woman well-known to us came in with her boyfriend, and neither of them was feeling any pain, as they had self-medicated with alcohol. He blew into the breathalyzer and registered extremely high. I let the machine rest and as I was bringing it toward her mouth it went off before she even got to blow into it! It never happened before, and I doubt it will ever happen again.

———◆◆◆◆———

People who live on the streets have one commodity that the rest of the world does not: they have time on their hands. Many roam around during the days or hang out in the library (some are incredibly well-read!). Others need a project to keep them alert and happy. Some are incredibly creative with their time and projects, more than many people could imagine.

I am going to tell you a story about a coat—not a technicolor dream coat, but still a wondrous creation by a friend with an idea and lots of time. We have many sleeping bags at our shelter to hand out to the folks who want to live by their own rules and not the rules of the shelter. One of our exceptionally brilliant guests asked if we had an extra bag that he could use for a project and we gladly gave him a puffy bright blue sleeping bag (the one he chose personally).

A few days later, he entered the shelter in a bright blue coat completely held together by silver duct tape. It looked pretty humorous on him. He asked if I would like to try it on. The second I put the coat on I started to heat up. It was by far the warmest coat I have ever worn. He had proven a point: "Looks aren't everything!"

We had a guest for years nicknamed "Grumpy." The other guests named him after the Snow White character but he was much taller, that was the only difference. If you said it was a beautiful day, he would try to convince you that it definitely was not! His glass was never half-full or half-empty, it was completely empty every time. He was well-liked in spite of this, though.

Our churches have automatic thermostats, so at times there can be a chill in the air. We have extra blankets for extremely cold nights. As I was leaving one night, he yelled out "Close the damned hall doors, it gets cold in here!" I said "That's odd, it's not like you to be grumpy." Naturally, the place fell apart in laughter, including him. We all want to fit in—we all want to be part of the gang.

"Grumpy" left this earth in 2015 at the age of 54. I can picture him in my mind saying "You call this Heaven? I thought it would be better than this.... I can't play a damn harp, what's wrong with you people!" Rest in peace, Grumpy!

———◆•▸◆◂•◆———

So many of our guests live on the fringe of society. Many times their language is peppered with profanity; sometimes by habit, other times by the anger of their situation. We try our best to keep that in check, especially when we are in the churches. I remember in the movie A Christmas Story that the narrator related his father was so eloquent in the art of profanity that it flowed out of him like poetry. We have a guest exactly like that: one single sentence could hold three to four completely unseemly words. When he was told that his language was unacceptable, he would reply "Oh man, I'm really ****ing sorry!"

This might look like he was being a wise guy and looking for trouble, but by the look on his face I knew that he hadn't realized what he said until after it left his lips. Besides his language and ridiculous alcohol abuse, he was a really likeable guy. He always told the truth.

One night, he helped an elderly guest up the hill to the shelter and when I asked him if he was staying he said "Hell no, I'm hammered; I will never pass the breathalyzer" and he left. His greatest ability was to make people laugh. That was a good gift for him to have because nobody could stay mad at him. He would also thank us for helping him, with his usual phrase "I love you, man."

Two separate times he was pulled out of snowbanks completely unconscious. Since my writings, we lost our friend to alcohol poisoning. He was only 34 years old. We all saw it coming over the years, but like an out-of-control freight train, there was no stopping it. At his service I read the following:

A female writer named L.R. Knost wrote "This broken world waits in darkness for the light that is inside you!"

We all knew the light he had inside of him; otherwise there wouldn't be so many people here to send him off on his new journey.

Please, don't have a drink in his honor, that's what killed him! Instead, help someone else who is in trouble in his honor.

Eastern religions call it Karma. We call it, "What goes around, comes around." Whatever you want to call it, spread around some good, some kindness, for humanity. But mostly, *do it for yourself.*

———◆◆◆◆———

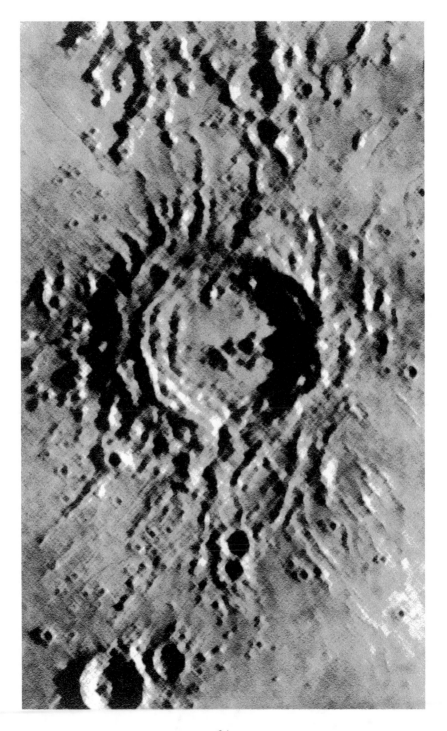

CHAPTER 2
The Hole

I dug a hole in my backyard
Put all my demons in a sack
Buried them deep as deep I could
They tried to dig their way right back
One holds drugs and alcohol
He smiles at me, and says I'm cursed
The next one tells me I'm no good
I had to bury that one first
I hear them whisper when it's quiet
They tell each other I am weak
But since the day I put them down
I am much stronger, it's strength I seek
Cause I dug a hole in my backyard
Put all my demons in a sack
For years and years I add cement
To make damn sure they don't come back

———◆•)⊗(•◆———

One winter night in 2008, a young couple arrived at our shelter saying that they had come to our small town to visit friends. When they went to leave, the roads had become icy and they knew that the roads would be too dangerous to drive on very soon. Folks at a local coffee shop told them where we were, and that it was within walking distance. They asked if they could stay and I told them certainly, we would have to fill out a little bit of paperwork then we could put them up for the night.

The young girl said they were very hungry and hadn't eaten since lunchtime, wondering if there was any food available. I told them that the church provided us with a space to stay but there was no kitchen available. I told them there was still a chance to find food. We entered the larger room where I had three homeless men staying for the night. They were all very familiar with hunger.

When I announced to these gentlemen that I had two hungry people who hadn't eaten since lunch, the backpacks and sacks hit the table immediately. Soon we had peanut butter sandwiches, beef stew, cookies, a Hershey bar, and a Twinkie that someone had sat on. These men had placed every item of food that they had on the table. They knew about hunger, but were willing to share all the food they had in their possession.

These men weren't bums, lazy people, or people who only cared about themselves. These were heroes without homes, warriors on the food front, people I was proud to count among my friends. Life never appears to be what it looks like. That's what I like most about it.

One night, a very young man came to the shelter and asked very politely if he could stay the night. He was well-groomed, talked quietly, and was extremely well-mannered. He told us he had lost his job and was far from his family with nowhere to go. We told him that was exactly why we had a shelter, and that he was welcome to stay and be part of our family for as long as the shelter months we stayed open for.

During the next weeks and then months of his stay he made some friends. Unfortunately, the people he was hanging out with were very heavy drinkers, so he was too. They had a camp on the edge of town, so on the warmer nights they stayed at the camp to drink, something they could not do at the shelter.

They found our young friend one morning, face down in a puddle only four or five inches deep. On the way back to his tent he had tripped and fallen. He was too drunk to lift his head and drowned. All who worked at the shelter were devastated, and have never really gotten over it to this day.

———◆◆◆◆———

A regular guest was telling a story when the shelter opened, and I was lucky enough to overhear it. He said he had seen a TV show on soldiers. Now, I don't have any proof, but I would bet there was a show on robots just before it!

He said, "You know all those soldiers over in Rack-Ran (Iraq and Iran combined), well they aren't really people, they are all robots! When a robot gets shot, two other robots put him on a stretcher and bring him to the robot hospital where the doctors put all the wires back in the right places and sew up that stuff that looks just like skin! When the robot wakes up there is a girl robot so he doesn't get lonely!"

This leads me to the conclusion that you can sit on your butt and watch Survivor on TV, or get off it and actually help people survive, while meeting folks ten times more interesting than you can see on television.

———◆◆◆◆———

A young male at the shelter was known to all as an intelligent, kind, and extremely bipolar guest who usually took his meds. One night while checking guests in, I noticed that his eyes looked different. I asked if he had been taking his meds that day, and he said he had, but I seriously doubted that.

I was staying the night there so I didn't make a big deal about it. At about 3AM, I woke up to the first karate shout, and saw him standing on one leg chopping at the air. Sounds funny on paper, but not so amusing when you wake up to it.

When I asked what he was doing, he said he was practicing his karate moves. I told him this was not the time or place for this, and that people were trying to sleep. He started to argue with me so I gave him options: lay down and go to sleep or do his karate out in the parking lot until the sun came up. It was 15 degrees Fahrenheit out, so he went to sleep. In the morning I reminded him to take his meds!

———————◆◆◆◆———————

I have learned a very important life lesson while writing this book: writing a book is a huge pain in the ass! I have written poetry since I was 10 and written music since I was 15, it was nothing like this. There are times that I have changed a few lines in a poem or rewritten a part of a song, but while writing this book I have rewritten some of the same chapters two or three times. I'm never quite happy with the way I word things.

I would not wish this job on anyone, and I now have a much greater admiration for many of the authors of books I have read and loved in my life. My hat goes off to every author that ever lived!!!!

One of my favorite writers and musicians, Tom Waits, probably put it in words we can all understand. His words were about writing music, but believe me, it goes for books too. He wrote "Writing music is like carrying water in your hands: by the time you get to the studio, you have nothing." That's exactly how I felt while writing down these stories: I was carrying water in my hands.

———————◆◆◆◆———————

A lot of our guests know that I write while I am at the shelter. Most of them see me when they get up to use the bathroom at night, or when they see the notebook and headlight on the table. When they ask what I write about, I tell them: sometimes poetry, sometimes stories I have witnessed, sometimes it's about you! They all smile at the last one.

A young man with a horrible drinking problem came up to me one night and asked if I would put something he wrote in my book. I read it and told him I would indeed add it. Here is what he wrote:

"Hello my name is *(redacted)*. Since I was born my mother loved me like crazy, she still does! She did the best she could for me, I was her first born. She kept my stomach full. On the holidays she made miracles. She was only 18 when she had me. I wish I could make her proud. It makes me cry when I think about it."

He had tears in his eyes when he gave me the note. We lost him a few years later to alcohol poisoning.

----●+)x(+●----

On an exceptionally cold night, a very large person in a parka with fur around the hood walked through our doors. All I could see was a pair of wire rimmed glasses. The person had a very deep voice and told me that a local man had told them where our shelter was for the month. The person asked if we had room for them, I said certainly, but we would have to take a minute to fill out some paperwork. The person was hesitant about that. I told them that any paperwork we had was kept by one of the coordinators and only used for homeless counts and used to make our lives easier by finding out what problems may arise. They consented, so I took them into another room for privacy.

When I asked for a name, I was given a very feminine one. My face must have shown my surprised as the woman said "You thought I was a guy, right?" I told her that the large parka made her look much larger than she was, not sure she bought that answer though. She proceeded to tell me that she would only be with us for a few days as she was traveling. I asked if it would be okay for her to tell me where she was heading. Without skipping a beat, she said she had friends in Arizona and Montana and had not made up her mind yet.

I hesitated a moment and said "Arizona is pretty nice in the winter, Montana is even colder than it is here right now!" She kind of looked at me like she didn't know what I was talking about, so I stopped pushing this grand idea. She left the shelter three days later without any parting words. We will never know the outcome. I like to picture her standing on a beautiful meadow somewhere in Arizona, watching the sun set.

———◆◆▶◀◆———

We lost another good friend of ours last night. He was a very intelligent man; he had an intense amount of empathy for others. He is another whose mind told him that the government was spying on him and would eventually track him down.

He stopped sleeping inside our shelter because he believed that some of our other homeless guests were really spies sent by the government to keep track of his every move. There is no way of talking someone out of paranoid thoughts once they believe their story is true. Maybe medication would help, but then he would think it was the government's idea to take control of him.

He would always stop by to visit us. We would beg him to stay, but it was futile: he was entrenched by his mental illness. He was found unconscious by another individual who was homeless. He left this earth six hours later.

———◆◆▶◀◆———

CHAPTER 3
Shadows

I hide in the alleys
In the shadows of town
It's not that I'm shy
They don't want me around
I hear whispers and laughter
Sometimes it's real
I am battered and broken
I may never heal
I try hard to be good
But I'm not good at that
The drinking and drugging.
I've got that down pat
I'm a jigsaw puzzle
Without all the pieces
An old dollar bill
That is torn and has creases
I live in your world
Full of laughter and lies
There must be a ghost
In these old haunted eyes
I stopped asking for help
There was no reply

We must try to remember, with all of our thoughts, that mental illness is listed as a disease. We don't treat it that way in America: we treat is as a defect or a personal choice someone is making. Many people make jokes about the way some of our folks at the shelter behave. Remember, if someone has cancer, a heart condition, diabetes, or any other medical disease, we don't hear people making fun of their conditions. With mental illness, though, it is open season.

I hope someday that will change. In some of the writings here I have shown some of that behavior in a humorous nature. I have hopefully not degraded any of the people I describe by doing that. I want to humanize the mental illness I see, not berate an individual for their behavior. Hence the title "Humor, Humility, Homelessness." Unfortunately, I can find humor in even the darkest of places: it's a gift!

———◆◆◆◆◆———

All the holidays are different since I have worked at the shelter. Thanksgiving was one of those days when the extended family would get together and eat until no one could move. Now, we are all aware how special this day really is! While we laugh, talk, and eat, even in our immediate vicinity others are not as fortunate. We are aware that many live outside with no food, no heat, and no future.

Sounds depressing, doesn't it? It's not for us, though. We are doing our best to change what we can, when we can. We are not the problem, but part of the solution. We also gain the reality to actually be truly thankful for that day. We no longer whine about things we don't have or things we can't afford. Jimmy Stewart was right: it's a wonderful life!

———◆◆◆◆◆———

One of our guests came in one night in a really good mood, and proceeded to tell my wife and I that the local drug store just gave him a credit card. My wife saw it, and having worked for a bank for years, told him it was actually a courtesy card so he could get discounts on sale items. He was very adamant that it was a credit card and that he could charge up to $500 on it.

We both told him how lucky he was (choose your battles!). Three days later in casual conversation, I asked him how the credit card was working out. He told me that someone who looked just like him had gone in and used up all his credit... never a dull moment.

━━━━◆◆◆◆◆━━━━

A female guest who got along with everyone she met asked me if she could speak to me in private. We stepped around the corner, where she told me that she hated being a rat and telling on people, but one of our heroin addicts had bragged earlier about doing heroin in our bathroom late at night. I told her she was not being a rat, she was keeping her house clean. This is where you live, it needs to be a safe place.

I waited about half an hour so nobody could put her in the picture, and walked over to a table where two heroin users were seated. I had always been as kind as the situation allowed, because I know the power that drugs and alcohol have on the mind and body.

I told them that the word on the street was that someone was using heroin inside our shelter. That is a crime that can get someone banned for a year! All the coordinators vote on punishments, and we all tend to be on the same page when it comes to safety inside of the shelter.

I then asked them to empty their pockets and backpacks on the table. One left immediately: I told him to not come back on my watch. I also informed the coordinator taking over on the next week.

━━━━◆◆◆◆◆━━━━

We always have homeless guests who are willing to help us out, even back us up if a situation is going badly. Whenever a brand

33

new overnight volunteer or couple show up, I will explain to them that there is always help within a few feet of them. I will introduce them to a few of our guests, telling them that no matter what they need, this person is willing to help. Sometimes it's a woman I will introduce them to (there are a few I've met who I wouldn't want to arm wrestle!). I tell them that whether it's medical or bad behavior, to always call 911 first and the coordinator second.

Problems at our shelter are few and far between. It is an incredibly safe place and we all strive to keep it that way. Unfortunately, in the homeless community you will bump into people who are very dysfunctional: this small percentage of the population are really their own worst enemies. It's always caused by over medicating themselves because of life on the streets, addiction, mental illness, or a combination of all of the above.

———◆◆◆◆◆———

I'd like to clarify that some of our guests are dealing with financial difficulties instead of the drugs, drinking, or mental illness. We had plenty of folks staying because they couldn't afford a hotel, motel, or renting an apartment. Minimum wage does not cover these "luxuries."

I have a story that shows how quickly a person's life can change. We had a middle-aged man show up one night asking if he could spend the night with us. He had been sleeping in his truck but it had become too cold to deal with. He had no vices except that he smoked cigarettes. He told us that he had a wife and two children but had just gone through a divorce. He worked two jobs for a total of 65 hours per week to support his family and his small apartment. The day after Christmas, the boss from his second job told him that, since the holidays were over, they wouldn't need him. He put his furniture in storage and started sleeping in his truck. There are many circumstances like this linked to our homeless problems.

Over the years at the shelter we have had landscapers, lawyers, carpenters, painters, railroad workers, store owners, salespeople, telemarketers, clerks, hairstylists, mechanics, bus drivers, care workers, wait staff, a forestry agent, production workers, and members of our armed forces. The list goes on and on. By looking at the list, you will realize the effects of homelessness on a grand scale. It can happen to anyone. The person right next to you could end up homeless. In worst case scenarios, you could be there too. I think we are sometimes aware of this but do not want to think about it. I believe it is the reason we distance ourselves from the homeless problems. It's someone else's problem.

"The problem of being unwanted, unloved, and uncared for is the greatest problem."

—Mother Teresa

When going into the shelter on a Monday night, the first night of my week on duty, I was approached by a lot of people complaining about a large guest who had a serious attitude problem the night before. He had gotten out of bed late at night, walking around telling people that if anyone messed with him they were going to get hurt. Unfortunately, the two volunteers staying that night never called their coordinator to come down. The guest would have been asked to leave immediately. The police would also have been alerted to the situation.

When he showed up that night, I met him at the door. I told him he would not be allowed to stay but that I would give him a sleeping bag. I told him he could use the bathroom and stay warm for another half hour until I left, then he would have to leave as well. He said that everyone was lying, and he started to puff up and swear. I told him the deal had changed, and he was to leave now. He said "Let's see you make me leave!" I told folks behind me to call 911 and tell the police that we were going to have a problem.

At that point, I noticed two people to the left and right of me in my peripheral vision. Glancing quickly side to side, I noticed two of my shelter guests, one on each side. The guy on my left is 6'4" and had arms like an orangutan. The guy on my right was a steel worker in his younger days, a Native American with long black hair and a massive build.

My tall friend asked the troublemaker how good his math was. He replied "What are you talking about?" and my friend and guest responded "I count three big guys over here and one big mouth over there, if I were you, I would leave now!" He did. The police showed up as quick as they could get there, as they always do. Our problem had left but they went to find him and tell him he was no longer welcome at our shelter.

———————◆◆◆◆————————

Over the years, we have had many coordinators help at the shelter. This story is about one of the quietest, laid back, low key men I have ever met. Not only did he work our shelter but on weekends he went to a local prison to do bible studies! We all loved this guy. Still, he wouldn't be in this book without a story.

One of our guests who was young and relentless would constantly tell stories about how great he was. He could do anything, his intelligence was off the charts, he could leap tall buildings with a single bound.

One night, I showed up to get the keys from the coordinator on duty as the next week was mine. When I came in, the young man was following this coordinator around, interrupting his conversations with other guests, going on and on. All of a sudden our quiet, caring coordinator completely lost it. "I know, I know," he screamed, "You are great, wonderful, all the girls love you, you will win every medal at the next Olympics, you should be President of the United States! Just shut up, do you understand 'shut up'? I sure hope you do!"

The room was quiet, everyone sat in awe. The most kind person who had ever stepped into our shelter had just verbally bitch-slapped the most annoying person in the room. It happened years before I wrote it down, so I can't be sure all the words are accurate, but if they were different, they were just as good.

The same guest told me that one of his girlfriends shot him in the back with a BB gun. I asked if she had to stand in a line for that. Sounds mean, but once again, he was getting on the only nerve I had left. Plus, it got a laugh!

———◆◆◆◆———

In a confined space with many people, few chances to bathe, and clothes that sometimes die of old age and abuse, the smells could often wake a dead man. As the winter rolls on, you can sometimes see these smells hanging in the air above a person, or so it seems.

Case in point: we had a tall young man with very large feet who must have been in love with his socks because he never changed them. On one particular evening, he pulled his giant boots off and I thought I saw a green mist rising off his socks. The tsunami effect of this was noticeable, as one wave of people after another left the area in a hurry. I took his boots and socks (not touching them directly) to the door, and put them outside. The following conversation really did happen.

I told him "Tomorrow, I will bring in Odor Eaters for the boots and sprays, lots of sprays. But if you don't change your socks before tomorrow night, you will not be allowed to stay in the shelter. Wash your socks in the sink if you want to, also wash those feet!" (Me doing my "Bad Daddy" routine)

He said "What?" I asked if his hearing had been affected by the awful smells coming from the boots. He replied "No." So I said, "Don't make me repeat what I just told you." The following night, all was well. The odors of good claimed victory!

———◆◆◆◆———

CHAPTER 4
Your God

Don't tell me your God
Could destroy all the world
To show us his power and might

Don't tell me your God
Doesn't notice the poor and the homeless
That are right in his sight

Don't just read the book
And say all the prayers
While hoping these people pull through

Come down to the shelter
Roll up your sleeves
And show us what your God can do!

———◆→◀◆◀◆———

Working inside the wonderful churches that keep all our guests warm, I sometimes find roadblocks and disrespect from people who call themselves religious. It is very rare, but the idea that everyone has to be on the same team or think the same ideas never sits well with me; it never has, even when I was younger and went to church.

When asked what church I belong to, I answer that I am multi-faith, and more spiritual than religious. Many people understand what I'm talking about, but those who don't can have pretty obnoxious answers: "I'm sorry I won't see you in Heaven, you seem like a good guy!" or "You need to come to my church and learn the truth!"

I already know my truth. My truth has come slowly throughout my lifetime. From Christians, Jews, Muslims, Taoists, Agnostics, Buddhists, Hindis, and most of all the Native cultures of the Americas. I try to find the things in each one that make sense to me, teaches me, and puts hope in my soul.

I have read many spiritual philosophies that basically say "There are many ways to cook an egg. None of them are wrong. I do not have to choose just one! They are bowls full of candy, each with its own taste, each with its own wonder. They can lead to enlightenment. In the wrong hands, they can lead to death and war. If you have never opened your mind to all of life's possibilities, then you should definitely not judge others."

I am writing this because I am upset. Tonight I was told that I would not see any afterlife by a supposed Christian. At first I was angry. Many of the philosophies I have read told me to let that anger go, to not keep it inside me or I would be the only one hurt by it. I believed that to be true, so I followed that advice.

My final words on this: never let others decide what you should do with your life. Follow your heart, walk through nature when you are upset and you will find what is true to you. Stick to whatever you feel is real. If you find a religion or spirituality that helps you through this world, I am happy for you. I respect your choice; please remember to do the same. Amen.

———◆◆◆◆———

The book you are reading is composed of notes and stories I wrote while I was at the shelter overnight. The next thing you will read was not written by me: it was written by a local reporter named Brian Koonz. This story is so moving that when it came out years ago, I cut it out and framed it on my office wall so anyone who came in could read it.

I tracked Brian down to see if I could get permission to add it to my book. He graciously said yes, and was excited about this book. Brian has moved on to being an Adjunct Professor of Journalism at a local college. I am thrilled that he allowed me to use this incredible story. It is appropriately titled, "I Saw the Face of God That Day" from his "Take On Life" column in the *Danbury News-Times*. People's names were used in this story because they were already used in a newspaper. *(Reprinted with permission from Brian Koonz)*.

Michael Oles had never seen a complexion quite like the one he saw that night four or five years ago at the Dorothy Day House shelter on Spring Street in Danbury.

As he looked into Michael Kusen's vacant face, the bearded man's skin wasn't exactly gray. It was closer to chalky, maybe even a little bit ashen, like the contents of a spent backyard grill.

"It was brutally cold and there was all kinds of snow on the ground, kind of like the winter we're having now," said Oles, a deacon at the Church of St. Mary in Bethel who volunteers at the shelter.

"I had seen Michael around before, but this time I was really worried about him. He didn't look so good. We only had 16 beds and a few more people than that had already lined up. Somebody was going to be left out."

So Oles held a makeshift lottery, just like he does every time there aren't enough beds to go around. Moments after Oles called out the last number, he watched Kusen disappear into the darkness.

Kusen came back the next night with the same, starchy complexion. Unfortunately, all the other homeless folks looking to elude winter's grip came back, too.

Once more, Oles pulled out 16 numbers and awarded each winner a bed for the night. Once more, Kusen found himself on the outside looking in from the cold.

"On the third night, I saw Michael again. He looked worse than ever," Oles said. "For a minute, I thought about rigging the lottery so he could get a bed, but something inside told me not to do it.

"Sure enough, Michael's number was called and he finally got a bed. As I'm getting everyone settled in, I feel someone poking me in the back. I turned around and it was Michael. He told me, 'I can't stay here.'

"I looked at him and said, 'What do you mean you can't stay here? Get in bed. Get a good night's rest.' But he kept at it. Finally, he told me there was a woman outside who needed a bed more than him."

Now, when Oles looked into Michael's face, he didn't see pallid suffering. He saw something deeper, something beautiful and spiritual and profound.

"I saw the face of God that day," Oles said.

Although Kusen insists he was just doing "the right thing," Oles will tell you Kusen taught him about the humanity of homelessness that night.

"There was so many nights when I was out in the cold," said Kusen, a Vietnam War veteran who lives in his own apartment in Danbury these days. "It was a very hard life.

"But as hard as it was for me, I couldn't leave that lady outside. I didn't know her or anything. I had never seen her before. But I knew I had to give her my bed."

Kusen said there are lots of homeless people in Danbury who refuse help, people who walk under society's radar and sleep in the city's shadows, even on the coldest of nights.

"We have a lot of good agencies here to help (homeless) people, but they can't do it alone," Kusen said. "Everybody needs to help each other. The agencies need volunteers and they need funding."

Just about every morning, the 62-year-old Kusen volunteers at the Dorothy Day House to help the less fortunate, to show them that life can change for people without shelter, or even, a winning lottery ticket for a bed.

Kusen still has that long flowing beard, a straggly storybook he wears on his face to remind him of those painfully cold winters of years past.

"Right now, I'm sitting home watching TV and I'm nice and warm," Kusen said Thursday afternoon. "But it wasn't always like this. I was on and off the streets for a long time."

There's a Bible verse from Hebrews on the Dorothy Day website that reads, "Do not neglect to show hospitality, for by that means some have entertained angels without knowing it."

If you don't believe me, just ask Michael Oles.

———◆·▸◂·◆———

Inside of our shelter, we all become witnesses. We witness people fighting for survival, their sanity, from wars they can never stop fighting, from mental and physical abuse from others, from alcohol and drug addictions. Mostly, fighting to fit in anywhere in our society. We also witness acts of kindness on a much grander scale than normally seen in this great country of ours. Acts of kindness, selflessness, and even courage.

Because the local churches are kind enough to give us a space each month to keep people safe and warm, many of our volunteers are members of different churches. That leads to people seeing things in different perspectives than they've become used to. The next story is probably one of the most moving ones you will read in this book.

An elderly female guest came through our door one night limping horribly. When asked about it, she told us that she had lost her shoes. Another homeless woman had given her the extra pair of shoes she owned, but unfortunately those shoes were one size too small for her. When she took off her shoes, her feet were raw and blistered.

A Christian female coordinator jumped into action. She came out of the Ladies' Room with a plastic pan full of warm water. She proceeded to get down on her knees and slowly, carefully wash our guest's feet. She looked up at us and told us that this is what Jesus would do. She wasn't wearing a WWJD bracelet, she was actually doing it.

I am no longer affiliated with any one religious organization. My belief system is my own and very personal, but I am aligned with all the people I work with whose hearts and souls carry out the teachings of great religions. This sort of action reflects all the great ideas I've read about which shape my spirituality: we need to focus on what makes us alike, not on what makes us different.

I was very moved watching a human act with conviction and faith to help another who was in so much need. In a big world, the little things count. She was helping one woman while healing everyone in the room who watched her.

If you decide you want to help out at a homeless shelter, there are some simple things you should be aware of. People who are long term shelter guests have usually gained an intuition while living on the streets. If you are afraid of them, they know it. If you feel sorry for them, pity them, or look down on them, they know it. If you are serious about making their lives more tolerable and keeping them warm at night, they know that too.

The games we play in our society trickle through their fingers like sand. They deal with the reality of getting through one more day. Even those with dementia or serious mental illness can figure out who is trying to help them and who is just going through the motions.

Talk to the homeless as you would any other human beings. Help them, but let them know you will not meet disrespect with excess kindness. Just as in all human relationships, sometimes you help them up, sometimes you establish firm boundaries.

Providing 'special treatment' because someone doesn't have a place to live is a masked type of pity. We all make our own weather, sometimes calm, other times stormy. We do not deal with stormy weather inside the shelter. When it is calm, everyone feels safe and sleeps better. The stormy weather goes outside where it belongs. It does get a low-temp-rated sleeping bag on the way out the door!

When an overnight volunteer complained to me about having to put someone out on a cold night, I told him that in my job description I sometimes need to leave my compassion and empathy for a single individual outside the door. Since we are an all-volunteer shelter, who will come back to help us if anyone inside is attacked or injured? It is serious business securing a shelter.

These next stories are about a nature-loving homeless man who sometimes had a problem with reality. He is non-violent, very polite, but does have some strange habits. He is obsessive-compulsive, always doing things in sets of three. But he also eats nature! Sometimes leaves, or the bark from a tree, but he seems to especially like roots.

In one of the churches kind enough to put us up, he lifted a small plant out of its pot, snapped off a root, and ate it. I told him that some roots are poisonous and can kill you! He smiled politely and said "Not yet."

Another time, I saw him in front of a coffee shop. He reached up and grabbed a tree branch and slowly proceeded to dip it into his coffee cup for about thirty seconds. He smiled as if he had accomplished something amazing; I will never really know what he was thinking. The two answers I came up with were:

- he was giving the tree a drink of his coffee, or
- he was making his coffee tree-flavored.

Either of these work for me. To me, it was a strange event. To him, it was his reality. He has since found his sister and an apartment. He is a much happier soul.

On a different occasion with the same guest, Shower Day! I was talking to a young guest who was the father of a three year old boy. While we were talking about children, my nature-loving friend said, "Kids are great." I then asked him if he had any. He looked nervous and said, "A couple." I asked him what their names were and he blurted out, "Come on man, I was just trying to fit into the conversation!" Everyone started laughing and he smiled too.

In these pages, you have read many stories of generosity in the homeless community. I am always amazed at how eager the homeless are to help one another. We all have generous people in our communities and in our society, but it pales in comparison to the acts of kindness coming from those with little to share.

One of our guests came in on a Friday night very depressed. He sat alone in a corner with his head down and talked to no one. This was unusual behavior for this particular person. Another guest approached him to find out what was wrong. He explained that Saturday was the only day he could visit his son, but he had lost his bus pass and did not have enough money to buy another.

Word passed through the shelter. Soon people were walking by the table he was sitting at, emptying their pockets of pennies, nickels, dimes, and quarters. There was enough change to allow him to visit his son. Imagine a world like that!

———◆◆◆◆◆———

I still consider myself a child of the Sixties Generation and a child of the world, only now this child has grown into an old man. The shelter keeps me acting and feeling much younger than the years I have been here. When we look into the eyes of a child, we see innocence and acceptance. A child will accept ideas, faith, skin color, physical ailments, the list never stops.

Children learn to be untrusting, they are taught to be bigots or racist, to show violence and hatred, and to fight. I learned some of this very well myself, especially the fighting part. I was an angry child for good reasons. The Hippie Movement started to change my behavior—the shelter has continued that lesson.

I have become more childlike. I do not judge, I accept all faiths, someone's appearance doesn't matter, only the behavior of the person inside. I am not afraid or offended by others' sexuality, as they are harming no one. I try not to hate. I will only fight when all other options are gone. The shelter helps heal me. For the first time, I am comfortable in my own skin.

Ernest Hemingway had the best quote for this. "Perhaps strength does not reside in never having been broken, but in the courage to grow strong in broken places."

———◆▸❌◂◆———

CHAPTER 5
Spitting Out The Poison

My heart has an ache
It cannot take this sorrow
I'm afraid it just might break
Do you have one I can borrow?

Give me a heart that doesn't care
And some eyes that come with blinders
Send my soul out on vacation
To a place with no reminders

Of the things I cannot change
The homelessness that taunts me
The things I can't unsee
The way it always haunts me

I'm not asking with no reason
I'm not begging you to hide me
I'm just spitting out the poison
So it doesn't stay inside me

Many people I've met in my life started out unsure, scared, confused, or damaged by their childhood. Many create personas or characters who are bolder, stronger, more fearless than they could possibly be. They wear these personas like a suit of armor to protect themselves from a world they are unsure of. I know because I was like this from my own childhood.

Surprisingly, as they age they absorb these suits of armor into their personalities and it becomes part of who they really are. It seems that the secret to living a normal life is to accept the fact that while you created something to protect yourself, you actually changed your own personality with it.

You are now stronger, funnier, fearless. All because you stopped hiding behind a damaged psyche and inadvertently pushed yourself forward to self-confidence. Look into the mirror and be proud of your accomplishments.

One of our guests who had problems with alcohol and anger management was asked to leave because of his aggressive behavior towards another person staying with us. When I left the shelter, he was outside sitting on the sleeping bag I had given him.

He apologized to me for lashing out at me when I was putting him out for the night, saying I had always treated him better than most people did. I asked if he wanted to go have a cup of coffee with me and talk. He did. It didn't take long to figure out the kind of behavior he exhibited every time he got drunk.

He told me that his father was a Vietnam veteran who had seen quite a bit of action in the jungle. Every once in awhile his mother would scream out in the middle of the night for him and his younger brother to hide. His father had woken up and gone to the closet to get his loaded gun out. His PTSD put the whole family in danger.

I told him that since he shared this story with me, maybe he could visit with a friend of the shelter who helped people sort out problems. He said he wouldn't talk to a "shrink." I told him that the woman just wanted to help people out and did not charge for it. He declined the offer. It also seems his younger brother had similar problems, only he used heroin instead of alcohol.

I believe that sometimes a simple set of words can make you realize how you can move your life forward and cancel out some of the things you've done that you are not proud of. Carl Jung taught me that lesson with this quote: "Knowing your own darkness is the best method for dealing with the darkness of other people."

In the military, medical field, police work, and other high-stress jobs where humans have to deal with the devastation and tragedy of others, we see high numbers of people dealing with PTSD. I believe many of our homeless are dealing with the same thing, many from traumatic childhood memories. Instead of walking through a minefield like a solider would, they are walking through mindfields where a certain smell, sound, or sight triggers a memory that they'd rather not recall.

I have that same PTSD. Many people praise you when you work to help others, not understanding that the help works in both directions. I try to help our guests navigate through problems when I can, and in turn, I recognize that I have been there myself and can now move further ahead through my own journey.

The most successful folks will stop self-medicating with drugs and alcohol so they can get a much cleaner picture of what needs to get fixed to have a more productive and joyful life. Any of the shelter staff and my friends from the homeless community who may be reading this, thank you for helping me be a better human!

A quote from one of my favorite authors, Theodore Geisel (a/k/a Dr. Seuss):

> You have brains in your head
> And feet in your shoes.
> You can steer yourself
> In any direction you choose!

Some excellent advice for all of us!

We see many veterans of many wars at our shelter. Bad times during brutal wars change people drastically. We had an elderly Vietnam era veteran with us for a couple years. We loved having him with us because he was very vocal when people were being idiots. He would yell out "These people are all volunteers, they didn't get paid to babysit you! Go to bed, or get out!" I used to say the same thing, only he did it much louder! He served two tours in the Navy supplying small boats with food and munitions going up the rivers. They saw a lot of action and were targeted many times.

Women with children get the first chance at housing, and that's the way it should be. But what about our veterans? They either wait a long time for housing, or are told that they have immediate housing 50-100 miles from their friends and family. I don't think I have ever seen a veteran take that deal.

One night in a bout of depression our guest told me, "I went to church, I raised my family, I went to war for my country, now I will die on the streets homeless and nobody will miss me!" Soon after that statement, a room opened up in a housing project in our town. When the director heard the story, she gave him the room. All is well with him, but we need to do more for our veterans.

On the brighter side, there are large pharmacies out there that will supply all of a veteran's medical needs with the right paperwork, if they cannot afford it. Make sure any veterans you know are aware of this. I only found out because the veteran I am talking about was taking his heart medicine every other day because he could not afford to buy more.

———◆◆◆———

Drug addiction, alcoholism, and mental illness are not taken seriously for what they really are. A horrible, life-changing wrecking ball that destroys everything in its way. An illness with very few answers.

When entering our shelter the first time every year, we have questionnaires that have to be filled out. This helps us deal with people better by knowing problems ahead of time, as long as people are truthful.

When asking someone if they have problems with alcohol, many say yes. When asked about drug problems, fewer will say yes, mostly because it's illegal. When asked about mental problems, 90% say no. This is the stigma our society has created for those in need asking for help. If we can't change this, our future will only see more of the same.

This country really needs to start treating mental illness with more dignity and understanding. For those whose minds, usually through no active choice on their part, lead them to constantly make bad choices and destructive decisions. We can do better, and we clearly have to for future generations.

Like I said in the beginning of this book, I have no training in psychology or psychiatry. However, when you spend years upon years creating working agencies within this space, and see the same problems coming up to slap you in the face every night, you would be a fool not to notice them. We can't keep throwing money at these problems and think that's an effective answer! Instead, we need to hire more people (especially in large cities) to try and lead people in the right direction. The best idea I have seen is a program called "Housing First" at **endhomelessness.org**.

Christmas is supposed to be a time of joy. Inside a shelter, it can be a very humbling time of year. People miss their families; they miss the life they used to have more than ever. One of the churches we stay at has children's classes during the day. We use those classrooms during the night. When working in a position with other coordinators and volunteers, we need uplifting moments to push us onward, to make us all want to be there.

About eight years ago I was letting our guests into a church classroom on Christmas Eve. People were in good spirits, but still thinking about what their societal status was. When entering the classroom and switching on the lights, the most wondrous thing happened: we were standing in the very middle of Christmas! The teachers and the children had decorated, not for them-selves but for us. There were Christmas lights, a small tree, handmade cards and stockings with everyday necessities and candy. Under the tree were warm socks (new ones!), sweatshirts, and long johns.

Christmas had come to our town, to our people, to our shelter, and these wonderful people have kept it up to this day. Another one of our churches stays open all day Christmas and New Year with food, a TV, DVDs and plenty of company coming and going all day. A great thing, because so many of our folks have nowhere to go. That day, we also invite the folks who are considered to be poor, and anyone else who has no place to go. I believe this is the true spirit of the holidays!

Telling you uplifting moments is extremely rewarding to me, but I usually have a flip side to all the stories. Two years after our Christmas Eve awakening, we had the same set-up in the church with lights, tree, Christmas cookies, and lots of new clothes.

A young guest in her late twenties was staring at a beautiful red-hooded sweatshirt with a sparkly design on the back. The church had asked us for sizes and how many men and women we had, so this sweatshirt belonged to her. I told her she should try it on; she turned to me with tears in her eyes and said "I don't deserve it. The state took my children away, I am a bad mother."

I did my best to convince her that she did deserve it and if she worked really hard, she could get her life and children back. I have been humbled at the shelter many times. I believe the time of year and seeing such a broken-down person made this one the most humbling. I walked out into the hallway. I could not let certain people there see the tears in the corners of my eyes. It would be like bleeding in front of a shark.

CHAPTER 6
Ghosts

I see ghosts
People I once knew
They stand outside the shelter door
Trying to come in once more
Ragged, ravaged, weather worn
Some wishing they were never born
I see ghosts

I feel ghosts
Never ever far away
Tugging on my untucked shirt
Telling me how much they hurt
Asking if I'm one who cares
Or looks through them like no one's there
I feel ghosts

I smell ghosts
Floating with the breeze
Stale alcohol from real strong drink
Of those who bathe in bathroom sinks
Clothes that scream for laundry soap
Worn out socks that have lost all hope
I smell ghosts

I hear ghosts
Whispering in dark corners
Of days gone by, the things they miss
How did it ever come to this?
Lost in time, broken voices
Wishing they could change their choices
I hear ghosts

The most haunting thing of ghosts I've met
Is that some of them are not dead yet

On a very stormy night at the shelter, a young male guest came in soaking wet, so wet you could have wrung him out like a sponge. The good news was that the church we were staying in had started gathering clothing for the poor and homeless and kept them in a walk-in closet on the first floor. It was named in honor of one of our homeless guests who always helped everyone he ran into. I took the young guest downstairs to pick out dry clothes and shoes. There was a bathroom nearby where he could change.

While picking out clothes, he told me he was used to being wet and cold. Whenever he made his father mad, he was forced to stand outside in the rain or snow until his father decided he could come inside again. When he went to change, I thought to myself that there were times I could have done better raising my children, but that night I was the best father in the world!

Many people live in dark rooms, rooms inside their head where horrible abuses happened, whether physical, mental, sexual, or neglect. If you don't confront these nightmares you will always be in that room. If I get the chance, I will tell people that they need to get out of that room and slam the door behind them. Triggered memories will always push you back inside, but the more you fight to get out, the easier it is to slam the door.

Build a new room, paint it your favorite color, put the paintings on the wall that you like. Find friends you can trust, family you forgot or pushed away. Make things new again. Most of all, live in the moment and stop self-medicating with drugs and alcohol, because it has never given you freedom. Living in the past ruins the future: you lose, your abuser wins. Don't let that happen!

I am reminded of a quote by the famous cinematographer Werner Herzog, "All of us are in some sort of theatre that we create for ourselves."

One of the guests in our shelter ended up being a close friend and a like-minded soul. He was a sponge for knowledge, and we talked about many things. He was also a heroin addict. He would stay straight for long periods of time, then he would slip. When he was sober, he drew the most magnificent artwork. He laughed and told jokes that made all of us laugh. He was an amazing person to know and to be around.

He eventually screwed up enough to end up in jail. We wrote each other while he did his time. He told me he was taking all the drug courses available and was done with heroin. I was thrilled to hear it. He was finally let go after completing his sentence. He got a job and everything looked wonderful. A woman who knew his family had given him a room until he could afford his own place.

About two weeks after his release I received a call that they had found him in his room with the needle still in his arm. He died during the night of a Fentanyl overdose. I walked into my garden that night and sent him a prayer from all the religions in the world, from all the Native cultures that I so respect, from all the people at the shelter who grew to love him, from my wife and myself.

He is gone, but he is released from pain. He will live on in my memory until my journey ends. This is the reality and tragedy of drug addiction. It will make you lie to yourself. It will send you, with no hope, back to that dark room that you try to avoid at all costs.

When losing a friend like that amazing guest, I think back to a phrase I have heard all my life "When someone you admire passes away, they take a piece of you with them."

What I have never seen in writing is the fact that even though they took a piece of you with them, think of all the pieces they added to you while they were here.
- A joke when they knew your mood was dark after putting someone out on a cold night for disrespecting the shelter rules,
- A knowing look and saying "You had to do that, there was going to be trouble,"
- Watching them help someone new to homelessness with more kindness than I can explain.

These are the types of pieces that they have added to my life before the day they took a piece away.

———◆◆▶◀◆———

I have mentioned that on some occasions, people are asked to leave the shelter. One night, a young guest who we all liked was acting peculiar and hard to get along with. He was arguing with another guest and wouldn't stop when we asked him to, so he had to leave. He was given a sleeping bag and sent on his way.

The church we were staying at had a dumpster and a large recycling bin outside. In the morning, the maintenance worker went to dump a large amount of paper into the recycle bin. The next thing he heard was "What are you doing? I was sleeping in here!" He had found our wandering guest and had a scare to boot! So remember, folks: we need more help and better programs to get to those who need help: *Recycle the Homeless!*

———◆◆▶◀◆———

We don't allow anyone under 18 to stay at the shelter for many reasons, including insurance. One particularly cold night, a sixteen year old male came to us with a very noticeable black eye. He told us his father had caught him in the garage doing drugs and had flipped out on him. He had no other relatives or friends in the area.

I called the police department for advice. They said as long as they had his name and address he could stay with us for the night, and they would pick him up in the morning and try to figure things out with the parents. It seemed like a good idea and everyone would have time to calm down.

The boy would have to sleep next to the overnight volunteers, and if he had to use the Men's Room, one would have to go with him and wait outside the door. We have to be very careful not to jeopardize our standings with churches, police, families, and insurance companies. We need the shelter to work like a well-oiled clock.

While setting up his bedding, one of our older gentlemen who could never stay away from large amounts of alcohol said

"What's wrong, son, Daddy punch you in the eye? You got off easy. When I was twelve my father threw me through the closed window of my second story bedroom into the backyard. I went to school with a broken arm, separated shoulder, and cuts all over my face and arms and nobody even asked me what happened!" I realized we were not just dealing with adults with serious problems; we were dealing with damaged children who could never get over their childhood traumas.

———◆→×←◆———

Myths About Homelessness

1. The homeless are dirty and smell bad.

TRUTH: Many homeless people are very clean even though they have limited access to tubs and showers. Many will put a towel on the bathroom floor and clean themselves head to toe with a washcloth. The people I have met who have poor personal hygiene are usually extremely mentally ill and cannot care for themselves and have given up any hope of a normal existence.

2. The homeless are dangerous and violent.

TRUTH: Most are very easy to deal with; their levels of violence are not any different than those who have homes. You could most likely fact check this with police departments, who get injured more when they show up at homes where domestic violence issues have been called in. The stats are no higher or lower than the rest of the country.

3. The homeless are lazy and don't want to work.

TRUTH: More than 50% of the people we work with have full- or part-time jobs. Most are at minimum wage with no benefits. If they own a car, it is even harder to make ends meet.

People with addictive behavior will always put their money towards their addictions. Their body, their mind, and their emotions all tell them to do this, and at a certain point, there is nothing left inside them telling them not to. If people have hallucinations, they may have conversations with people who are not really there. Try keeping a job with that problem!

When we see people get better jobs, whether through a turn of luck or working harder and overcoming addiction in their lives, they can move forward in leaps and bounds within a very short time.

4. The homeless are thieves and liars.

TRUTH: Once again, the majority of guests I have met are very good people. Remember, if you are hungry enough you will steal, and if you have children who are hungry you will do it sooner. If we were all in that situation we would behave the same way.

I cannot make any excuses for drug addicts and heavy alcoholics, because they will lie about anything and everything to get a drink or a fix. No matter how honest they might have once been, honesty takes a backseat to addictive behavior. Remember, they are not lying just to deceive you; they are lying to feed an inner hunger that is far worse than a hunger for food. No one can understand this very well unless they have been there. There is no joy, no caring, only being. I told you this would be truth.

5. The homeless are uneducated—that's why they're homeless.

TRUTH: All the homeless guests I have met went to school; some graduated high school, some did not, but many intelligent topics came up in our discussions. It's amazing the kind of feedback that comes back across philosophy, space, medicine, mathematics, and don't forget politics.

We try to keep people from talking politics or religion inside the shelter, though, because so many folks can get riled up by it, just like you and I!

One of our steady guests graduated from a very reputable college, third in his class of 280 students. In his thirties, he developed schizophrenia and started to believe that the government was tracking him. When most subjects came up, he was by far the most intelligent person I had ever met. We avoided talking about government issues because he would get so upset he would have panic attacks.

He asked me constantly if I had ever been in the CIA or FBI. Eventually I finally said, "For crying out loud, if I had been in the CIA or FBI, don't you think after two years I would have had your ass in jail already?" He laughed out loud and we went out for a coffee after the shelter closed. He never asked me again.

One Christmas Eve, I asked him if he wanted to use my cell phone to call his children and see how they were doing (they lived out of state). He told me he couldn't, because his call would be tracked and the government would know where his kids were.

The solid belief in something that is not real is the worst part of a mental illness like this. He was such a wonderful man, and everyone in our small town loved him. Maybe not the guy who owned the bicycle shop, actually, because our guest would fix all the kids' bikes in town for free!

He was kind, he was a good listener, he was everybody's friend. When he died of heart problems, we filled an entire church to standing room only; this church is only that packed three times a year on Christmas Eve, Christmas Day and Easter.

He had three eulogies: one from the shelter, one from the people who feed the homeless, and one from the church. It was a moving testament to how someone with nothing can still impact a whole town by his behavior alone. I still miss him along with many, many others.

CHAPTER 7
Empty Places

Reflections in the mirror shattered
Priceless tapestries of time
Now torn and tattered
An empty room, no one sits
Inside this place
Sound becomes echo
Engulfing this space
Darkness pours through a window
Extinguishing light
Our eyes just see shadows
Till we lose all our sight

No one comes here
It does not matter
It's reflections in the mirror shattered

———◆▸╳◂◆———

All of my writing is done while I am at the shelter.

Tonight there is a symphony going on. One guest is snoring in B Flat, another snores in a beautiful diminished chord. In a far corner, someone is asleep mumbling under their breath, asking for someone's forgiveness.

Quiet nights here are rare and seem surreal when they happen.

I remind myself that without this shelter, all of these souls would be out in the freezing cold.

With that said and the cacophony of sounds, there is no place I would rather be except with my own family.

This is my other family.

———◆▸╳◂◆———

It's getting very late here at the shelter. It's going on 1 AM. I usually stop writing around midnight and get some sleep. Tonight, my mind is very active and wants to keep writing. I always let my mind have its way: being the boss, it has the right!

Tonight I am thinking about the universe that we have here in the shelter. When we look off into space we see that everything is revolving around everything else. The molecules in our bodies do the same.

So goes the shelter: people orbit each other every night. If someone has extra food, they become the sun for that evening, everyone orbiting around them. If one of our funnier folks is in a good mood or has good jokes, they become the center of the universe.

If a person new to homelessness comes in the door scared, confused, wondering how to survive their situation, the planets spin around them giving advice on where to eat, where to get more help, telling them they are not alone. This is our town, our solar system, our galaxy, this is our universe.

———◆◆※◆◆———

Again, it's very late and this has nothing to do with homelessness, this is just me ranting about things that drive me crazy:

If you've ever looked at the sky and wondered if there are other species out there, welcome to the club. Looking at the Hubble pictures, it seems almost impossible to think we are the only species in the universe. We have cool pictures now of craft that we don't believe were made on our own planet, and which can reach speeds far beyond the limits of things we've created so far.

People wonder why we have not met any of the creators of these vehicles. Look around you and you will see: we are a highly aggressive species. We kill one another for any number of reasons. We go to war over spiritual beliefs. We fight over borders, and the old send our young to die. People are killed over the color of their skin, their sexual orientation, or a disputed parking space.

After we look at ourselves, would we like to contact a species like us? We would keep our distance, or we would start a war with them. I like these alien people... they seem smart!

———◆◆※◆◆———

My childhood was not an average one. My father did his best to try and prove how useless and inept I was. Looking back, I believe his mother may have done the same to him. My job was constantly trying to avoid him and stay out of his way in a very small house.

The reason I write this is not for people's sympathy. If I could go back in time, I would not have changed it. The more he tried to break me, the stronger I became. I want to show, though, how this behavior is like dominoes. It runs through families like a wildfire.

Sometimes I wonder if major portions of my life have been trying still to prove my father wrong. The human psyche is incredibly delicate.

I was very lucky to marry a woman who had a stable childhood. I dread to think of the things I might have said to my children. Still, whenever I hear or see anything about childhood abuse, it strikes a chord inside me. I want to track abusers down and make them pay for what they have done.

The problem is, after working in a shelter as long as I have, I now realize that the chances are that most abusers were also abused as children. I am not excusing their behavior, or giving them a Get-Out-Of-Jail-Free Card. Just finally realizing that the children are suffering because their parents are still suffering.

Naturally, this is not the case in every abuse situation, but I am fairly confident that the percentages are pretty high. I fight these same battles in my life. I am in pretty good shape mentally (depending on who you ask!) but I am occasionally triggered by a certain sight or sound, and I can feel the anger rush into my head like it never left.

One of my good friends said "We are all dysfunctional in some way or another; embrace it, it's part of you."

People who are homeless can have a lot of ailments to deal with. The rough life they live, and poor access to nutritious foods, at times lead to many medical problems. The hospitals do their best to help our guests but even when they do get medicines, they sometimes lose them or forget to take them.

It's a hard life living on the streets. A large guest of ours came to the door one night breathing heavily. He said he had had problems breathing all day long. At the end of my shift, I drove him to the Emergency Room, where they admitted him for testing.

The next day, I stopped in to check on him. He told me he was never going to leave the hospital. The bed was comfortable, the food was great, and he had his own TV to watch. The only problem he had was that he yelled at the night nurse who woke him up to check his vitals. That didn't go over very well. He was released the next day, and I was expecting him to fake some separate illness to get his room back!

A female guest of ours who was sweet and kind to everyone around her had a fond attachment to a five foot tall stuffed Simpsons character. Everywhere she went; it came along for the ride. It got to be a problem for her because it was so large. It had belonged to a good friend of hers who had passed away.

While talking to friends of ours, we came up with a solution. With her permission, we clipped off a small piece of the stuffed toy and put it in a locket, so she could have part of it with her at all times without dragging it all around town!

It lived in my closet for one winter, and I would take pictures for her of the toy riding my motorcycle, walking the treadmill, and petting my dogs. We both had fun with it. Luckily, she now has housing, and the stuffed character has a safe warm place to stay.

By now, you have realized that we have some interesting characters in our shelter. The homeless don't have a lot of money usually, but when a little bit is available, the local Dollar Store is like a magnet. Having said this, I will tell you another interesting story.

One of our guests came through the doors one night with

two large frying pans, one in each hand. They would not fit in his backpack. I immediately asked where they came from (who wouldn't!). He told me he had gotten them from the dollar store.

I asked if they were heavy and he replied "A little." I next asked why he had bought them. He told me that they were cheap and "Who knows? I could be walking down the street and somebody could say, 'Nice frying pans—I've got bacon and eggs!' Then I would have frying pans and breakfast!"

Some characters at our shelter are more colorful than others. The most literal proof of this comes to mind in the story of a guest who, for a long time, owned a vintage clothing store. He sometimes dressed as if he just walked out of the 1940s or 1950s. Other times, it seemed like he had just walked out of a circus tent.

We all loved this guy, he wasn't hurting anyone with his wild fashion and was pleasant to be around. He did have a habit of finding the most unusual clothing you could imagine. One night, he walked through the door in leopard skin tights! One of our more creative guests said, "Hey man, I'm glad you won and the leopard lost!" It got a lot of laughs, even from the jungle man himself.

People in our shelter can get territorial when they see someone setting up their bedding in a spot they consider to be their own. The coordinators usually intervene to keep tempers down, and this usually works out fine.

One night, when a guest set up in his usual corner, many others started complaining about his odor. As more and more people complained, I made a visit to his area to check on him and see how bad it really was. It was horrendous! I started to question him because he was usually such a clean person.

That's when I noticed the garbage can a few feet away. As I walked towards the can, the smell got worse by the step. I held my breath and looked inside of it. Someone had thrown a fish sandwich into the garbage can, not even in a bag. I don't know how old it was, but I am guessing the fish had been out of the water since last century. I took the can out to the dumpster, and all was well.

———◆◆◆◆◆———

As I am writing this, we are about to close the shelter until next winter. It's the middle of April, and the weather is getting more comfortable. We don't have enough churches or volunteers to stay open all year.

Even if we did, all of us who work there think that it is more healthy to leave this space for guests to make choices about their future. Do they move to another shelter, try and get a job and an apartment, or live outside like our early ancestors did? These are all choices. People can become comfortable doing the same thing over and over, but it will never change their situation.

We also realize that our overnight volunteers, and even our coordinating staff, may burn out and not be able to continue in a year-round situation. We have wonderful guests who come to our shelter each year; we also have the "problem children," who aren't happy unless everyone around them is miserable. These are the type of folks who can try your soul. Even across a five-month period, they can get under your skin. I still wish only the best for all of them. It is time for us to rest up!

———◆◆◆◆◆———

CHAPTER 8
Saints & Sinners

Everyone I know's a saint
And all of them are sinners
You're either really good at both
Or you are a beginner.

Helping those who need a hand
That's humility and class
Next you're driving on the highway
Calling someone else an ass.

It must be human nature
Yet in nature it seems rare
We think about our actions now,
Then wonder why we care.

The rules are made for everyone
Though some think that's not true,
We make the rules and break the rules
In everything we do.

We all look in the mirror
In that glass we see a winner
Yet everyone I know's a saint
And all of them are sinners.

One of the wonderful advantages of doing any kind of volunteer work is the type of people who are doing it with you. Very few people volunteer to be noticed or for admiration. It is done simply to make another human's life more bearable. Mostly, it is a feeling inside telling you that it is the right thing to do: a moral compass.

Too much attention for volunteering feels creepy. I always tell people who are praising me a line from a young group of musicians called The Winterpills: "I'm fighting the good fight but I'm not your savior, all you need to do is look at my past behavior."

The term "saints and sinners" has been around for years, but I don't think I have ever met anyone who would vote for me to be a "saint" alone: I have always played both positions on the field. If you read things in here that make you think I am an extraordinary person, picture me getting on a motorcycle at 2 AM, leaving a bar when I was young, drunk as a skunk with a head full of cocaine, and closing one eye so I could ride home without seeing doubles of everything. Life balances as I grow older.

We have so many volunteers at our shelter. All of the ones I have met are doing the right thing for the right reason. They have empathy for others, they truly care, and you can see this in their actions. I'd like to tell you a story about each one but that wouldn't be a book, that would be an encyclopedia. (If you are under 35, look up 'Encyclopedia.' It was like the first website we had years ago!)

One of our volunteers comes to mind for this story. This woman was a nurse who started out in the maternity ward and worked there for quite a long time. She decided she would move on to another job for a change of pace, she chose hospice work.

When I asked her why she made that choice she said "I spent years bringing children into this world, I thought it would be right to help those with limited time on their way out of this world." That made so much sense to me, and I hold both her and her decision in high regard.

Another volunteer has hiked just about every major trail in the United States, from beginning to end. His stories could fill a book, and I would gladly read it! We also had a husband and wife who served in the Peace Corps. They traveled to so many parts of the earth, and helped countless people to have a better life.

We have so many volunteers from so many different walks of life. These are people who watch the news or read the papers, and instead of thinking about how sad homelessness is, they come to us to do something about it. I am inspired by the human beings who walk through our doors, by all our volunteers who make a huge difference, and by the homeless folks who face so much adversity in this world yet still trudge on to the future and hope for changes in their lives.

Abraham Maslow said "What is necessary to change a person is to change their awareness of themselves."

<hr/>

Most people say they want to help out any way they can. We have one man who makes breakfast for the homeless and poor every Saturday and Sunday at one of our local churches, with only one helper. He has been doing this, and paying for most of it out of his own pocket, for years. A local doctor comes in when needed to give free health exams. If someone needs more medical help, they are referred to his office, where they will not be charged.

Many people say they care, but when you see a few people doing so many things with very little help, you realize that the old saying is correct: "Talk is cheap!"

Many times during the winter, local people stop by the shelter with gift cards from local coffee places. One of the best ideas I learned from the internet was buying movie tickets for the holidays: there will be warm seats and something to watch for at least a few hours.

<hr/>

All of us at the shelter are celebrating a huge success story. One of our guests who had communication problems, and had been on the streets for a very long time, has finally received help.

His sister was living in another town quite far from where we are. We were not able to get him much help without having a family member involved. While communicating with a friend on social media, she found that her brother was here. Not only had she not known where he was, she hadn't even been sure that he was alive.

The great news is that, with her help, he has gotten support, medication, and an apartment. She got in touch with us recently to tell us that he now has a job and bought himself a bicycle to ride there! If you had spent any time with him only one year earlier, you would have thought none of this was possible. Little miracles, little flashes of light in the darkness today: all is well in the world.

———◆◆◆◆———

Most of us realize that humans have the ability to do strange things. I especially notice this when going through some of the donation bags that are left either on the doorsteps of the shelter or in my driveway near the basement door. Donations to our shelter are greatly appreciated, but I am struck by what people think we can use at a homeless shelter. Examples:

- A very large burgundy couch cover
- Children's clothes
- Disposable razors for shaving (which were clearly previously used)
- Dog toys
- An angora sweater (which was not really angora, but a black sweater covered top-to-bottom with white animal hair!)
- Most surprising: a bread maker!

A woman in her eighties showed up one night with a beat-up old electric blanket. I told her I was sorry, but we didn't take electric blankets. She said "Well, you'll take this one!" I looked in her eyes, and I took it.

I wonder how far ahead some folks think when they're leaving these donations. Sometimes they are not useful, but at least they're good for a laugh.

———◆◆◆◆———

Years ago, I was working at the shelter with someone who said to me "It's not our job to try and help these folks, our job is only to keep them warm for the night." My answer was "Then tell me whose job that is, because it should fall on everyone who has a chance to help them."

For the record, this was an overnight volunteer who didn't stay around very long. The majority of our volunteers are very committed.

In America, everyone talks about our homelessness problem. I personally don't think we just have a homelessness problem. We have mental illness problems on a much broader scale than we would like to admit, and we need a lot more people working in this field.

I have a ton of respect for people working in the fields of psychiatry and psychology. There are so many steps in the ladder for each type of mental illness. Therefore, you should never prescribe the same treatments for the same illness. There will never be a one-size-fits-all situation. Just getting one person back on the road to normality is a monumental task.

Taking in the domains of childhood abuse, neglect, sexual abuse, and other traumas, the human psyche is as fragile as an egg. The reality of the situation is that all the king's horses and all the king's men may not be able to put Humpty Dumpty together again!

I consider my mind to be stronger today than it ever has been. Yet it still tells me at times that I am not good enough, that I do things for personal gain and not truth. Imagine having these dark thoughts and doubts while being under the crushing weight of serious mental illness.

Following from the topic of Humpty Dumpty: while laying on my cot trying to fade off to sleep during a shelter snorefest, I thought of how weird the poems and stories we tell to children are.

We want our children to feel safe, but then we read them stories about bears, witches who eat children, wolves trying to get at three little pigs. We also sing to newborns "Rockabye baby on the treetop, when the wind blows the cradle will rock. When the bough breaks, the cradle will fall, and down will come baby, cradle and all!" Yeah, that seems safe.

Over the past sixteen years, writing down my poems and thoughts at the shelter has become very enjoyable for me. It allows me to put my words and ideas on paper as people sleep and snore all around me. It has actually become a form of connection or a Zen-like state. I tried to do this at home but I did not feel the same, it was very unnatural for me. These nights also lead me to think about things I normally don't.

For instance, isn't it strange that so many places around us have animal shelters where the animals have a safe place to sleep, eat, receive medical care and attention from volunteers who walk or play with them, yet it is such a struggle for this country to come up with good solutions for our homelessness problem?

Don't get me wrong: I have two dogs who are actual family members. I just wonder how long we will let this problem continue to grow. We spend more time and money trying to pretend we don't have a problem.

One of our guests at the shelter kept complaining of pains in his chest. I had not heard about it until I came in the following week. The Emergency Room at our local hospital will treat the homeless with no charge, but the fact that some will fake medical problems to get narcotics make these doctors think twice about prescribing any addictive drugs.

After about six days of being uncomfortable, our guest had a heart attack. They rushed him to another hospital which had specialists better suited to treat him. Being friends with him, I was the first to get his call from the hospital.

He told me he was feeling much better, and that they gave him a room but there was no bed in it. I told him that the hospital knew he was homeless so they expected him to sleep on the floor. He roared with laughter, then called me a few names I can't print here!

I mentioned earlier that treating people inside a shelter just like anyone else you know is important. When he came back to us, he told everyone in the shelter the story. There was a lot of laughter before bedtime that night.

———◆◆✕◆◆———

Homeless people are unpredictable: I have heard that said more times than I can count. The truth is that the majority of people I have met at the shelter (and that's a lot of people) are exactly like the rest of us. They have the same wants, needs, and dreams as anyone else. The only difference is that we have easier access to both hope and the avenues to accomplish our dreams, while those living on the streets find those same dreams unattainable.

I see homelessness as a type of swamp. When you first enter it, your feet get stuck in the mud. If you turn around quickly, you can still get out. After a few years, you are stuck up to your waist. Eventually, you are up to your neck in the mud, screaming for help. By that time, most ears have become deaf to your calls.

The good news is that the shelters, social services, and some of the government agencies can still pull people from the mud. To slow this problem down, though, we need a lot more boots on the ground.

———◆◆✕◆◆———

Arthur P. Palmer

CHAPTER 9
This Is Not All

A climbing comes
Before a fall:
There is no end,
This is not all.

From young to aged,
The timeless place.
From life on earth
To endless space.

From sands of time
To shifting sands,
From all mankind
To just one man.

There is no end,
This is not all,
I'll see you then,
You'll hear my call.

*(This will be read to all my friends and family
when it is my time to move on!)*

In the early years of my life, whenever I tried to make sense of who I was, I was always looking at myself from the outside. It seemed like I was watching someone's life unravel slowly and constantly. It was like living inside an Ingmar Bergman movie.

Until I started working on getting myself clean and sober, I had no idea what I was capable of and what I could accomplish by putting my mind to work. Instead of looking at myself from the outside, I turned to the inside where all the problems were actually hiding, and to all those behaviors inside that I didn't like.

Looking at myself from the outside was like looking at that person I see in the mirror when I brush my teeth. Sometimes I had no idea what was going on deep inside.

I feel like the way to get some changes made is to look at yourself as a closed garage. Until you open the door up and go inside, you have no idea what you want to keep and what you need to get rid of. Maybe some of these ideas just come naturally with age and time.

———————— ❖❖❖ ————————

I have mentioned that we have some very well-read people occupying our shelter space. Many times, especially on bad weather days, most of our folks are at the library. They really enjoy being on the computers, but it's a small library so they do not have a lot of them. They will either grab a good book, or nap in a corner that's out of the way.

One of our very well-read guests, sitting at a large table full of others, said that he had just finished reading Homer's Odyssey. That is quite an accomplishment. He wasn't quite finished though, adding "The problem in our world is that there aren't enough intelligent people." He then gazed around the table as if he was superior to the other guests.

Another quickly responded, "Hey Einstein, you drank so much today that you peed yourself again: I can smell it from way over here!" It was a full body slam of a reply, and it was true: I had noticed it when the guest signed in for the night. Too much alcohol creates a mathematical equation for acting stupid.

———————— ❖❖❖ ————————

As long as I'm talking about Albert Einstein, I feel the need to add a couple of his amazing quotes to this book. A lot of people have heroes who are make-believe, like Superman, Batman, etc. I always leaned towards real people, Einstein being among the top ten.

The first quote: "The world is a dangerous place to live, not because of the people who are evil but because of the people who don't do anything about it."

My favorite, though, was an answer to a reporter's question. When asked to explain relativity to people who were not as intelligent as he was, he said "Put your hand on a hot stove for one minute and it seems like two hours. Sit with a nice girl for two hours, and it seems like one minute! That's relativity."

———◆◆◆———

This is another story about homeless children, only these children are living in Africa. One of my nieces traveled to Africa with a loving friend to help install water systems to connect to sources far away from remote villages. She was so impressed by the people she met there, who were hunter-gatherers like in many tribal villages. Whatever they hunted or found growing was placed in one big pot in the center of the village. Everyone shared, and I'm pretty sure there were no picky eaters present.

My niece told me that they owned very little, but were the most happy people she had ever met. If one person started singing, they all sang and danced together. She was amazed by their kindness and love. She later found out that many of the village women were not happy with their new water system. It seemed that in their long walks to the river, they could gossip about their in-laws and husbands! So it seems some behaviors are universal.

Traveling back to the airport in Africa, she met a woman who took in orphans. This woman would go to a local butcher and collect animal bones. She would then boil them to make broths they could use to make soups.

When the broth was finished, the bone would be laid out to dry. After drying, the bones were cut into small sections. The holes in the middle were filled with glue, and a can opener was inserted. The kids took them to town to sell to tourists. At my niece's wedding, every guest left with a bone can opener. Every time I use mine, I think of this wonderful woman and the children she is saving.

———◆◆◆———

One of my friends and fellow coordinators told me that there was a problem the previous night with a new guest who had talked about guns and knives when he got inside. He had also stared down some other guests and made them uncomfortable. We both went in the next evening to talk to him, asking him to come outside to chat.

He immediately became aggressive and wanted to know why we were singling him out. We told him that talking about weapons and intimidating others was not acceptable. He became more aggressive, so we told him he had to leave. He walked up the stairs to the sidewalk, turned to us with a glare and said "I'll be back, and I'm gonna bring my sister with me!"

We stared back at each other, trying not to laugh. How do you possibly respond to a threat like that? These moments of aggression are few and far between, but we do know how to deal with them. I sure hope that I never meet his sister.

Whole Lotta Shakin' Goin' On

As I have mentioned, we come across various forms of mental illness. Different types, levels, and conditions, so you never have exactly the same situations. At least I am never bored.

I have also talked about going into someone else's world when you know they can't come into our own. I'm a little twisted from the Sixties and I enjoy weird situations, so sometimes sending my mind on a vacation is natural for me, which leads to the next story.

Mental illness sometimes doesn't show up in a person for days at a time, other times, it is a tidal wave washing over them and dragging them away. The minute I saw our guest come through the door, I could tell he was underwater. Conversation was hard, but I needed to know if drugs were involved. They weren't.

He was restless, and his eyes kept darting from place to place as if he thought someone or something was after him. I reminded him that we run a safe shelter and that he would be able to get some much-needed sleep. He never heard a word I said, or at least he didn't seem to. After lights out, he kept getting up and moving to new spots around the church floor. It is a basement area with large support columns. Every fifteen minutes, he moved to a different column.

I finally got up to find out what was wrong. He told me that the minute he laid down next to a column it would start to shake, and he was afraid the building would collapse. I knew it was time for me to switch to another dimension. I told him that all of the columns he slept near were by the furnace, and its vibration could make them shake. I pointed to the other end, and told him those columns were far away from it and didn't shake at all. That was not true, but he fell asleep almost immediately after. Mission accomplished.

———◆◆◆◆———

There is a quote by someone I admire that I felt compelled to add to this book. I believe it fits very well into the homeless community, as many of our guests have travelled very rough roads in their lifetime. Henry Rollins is a punk/metal rocker who has become a philosopher for the new generations. When asked by a reporter "What kind of juice would you be and why?" he responded:

"I'd be olive oil, which is olive juice. Basically when they say it is 'cold pressed,' I imagine a bunch of olives between two pieces of cloth being mercilessly smashed. From that great pain and compression comes this ooze that is quite good! So I wouldn't be a fruit juice, I would be this heavy viscous liquid that is in the process of being smashed. I'm the product of violence, compression, and being stifled and I've got an amazing shelf life!"

Thank you, Henry, for teaching me what juice I would be too.

———◆◆◆◆———

CHAPTER 10
I Was Born For This

Abused, bruised, and battered
She stands before me

"I was born for this."
No love, no laughter,
No place to run.

God wants me to suffer
Just like his son.

A tear slowly falls.
Escaping her face.
It is all my fault,
I did not know my place.

She looks forward to pain.
Clouds, lightning, and rain.

From the moment she wakes
To look up at the sun.

She tells me her God
Is a merciful one.

There is nothing to change,
Not a thing she can do,
"I was born for this,"
She believes it is true.

————◆◆✕◆————

Not all the homeless people I have met were inside a shelter. On a vacation in Maine, my wife Ellen and I stopped at a sandwich shop to pick up some lunch. The weather outside was not the best for vacationing: it was dark, overcast, and raining steadily.

As we hurried across the parking lot toward the door, I noticed an elderly woman wearing a garbage bag as a raincoat. She was picking up small pieces of paper, some leaves and other small items, and putting them in her pockets. I realized she was most likely homeless, and possibly mentally ill. I told my wife to go ahead and I stopped to talk to her.

It was then that I noticed all the families and couples walking by and looking the other way so they would not have to feel guilty for avoiding her on purpose. I have seen many uplifting things in my life, but this moment was not one of them. I felt contempt towards everyone there who did not see this moment for what it was: another human being needing help.

I do not understand how people could walk by a person when it was so obvious that she was in trouble. When I talked to her she was very sweet, like she could have been anyone's grandmother. I asked her when she had eaten last, but she didn't know. I told her the sandwich shop had warm soup and really good sandwiches inside, but that she would need to leave her raincoat outside. I slipped some money into one of her hands.

She reached out with the other and as she touched my arm she said "Thank you" in a way that broke my heart. I had not done enough: I would leave her behind like the rest of the world had. The day became even gloomier, and it fit my mood. I have always been aware that I can't change the whole world or the injustice in it. I think the small personal incidents are the hardest to walk away from.

———●▸❈◂●———

A woman in her mid-thirties came to our shelter and stayed about three weeks. You could not move quickly, talk loudly, or even look in her direction sometimes: she would quickly hide her face inside the hood of her sweatshirt. My wife dealt with her because I am not very quiet, and often talk with my hands. We both believed that she had been terribly abused for many years.

I always wonder what can cause a human to do such terrible things to others, especially those people who are not as strong physically and mentally. After three weeks with us, she just stopped showing up. We both hoped that she had reconnected with someone in her past who treated her well, and not back to her abuser.

We see many males who faced abuse also, but most of them were children when it happened. Please! If you know or see someone being mentally or physically abused, report it to authorities. It will help our society, and especially the one being abused who needs help the most.

We had a woman in the shelter for about three years who had taken a bad fall and hit her head. She had permanent brain damage. She was clean, she treated everyone kindly, and smiled all the time. We all embraced having her in our shelter. The brain damage slurred her speech and affected her balance. She stumbled quite often, and sometimes fell down.

The laundromat in our town would let the homeless sit in their chairs on very cold days (depending on who was on duty that day). She was thrown out of there, and every store in town, for being drunk. I never saw her drink, there was never alcohol on her breath: it was a medical situation. Fortunately, she has found housing and does not have to deal with this anymore. No matter the story, the facts are more important than surface appearances.

Looking back at my life, I realize what a lucky person I am. I stepped into drugs and alcohol at a very early age, and could have lived a wasted life as a result. Luckily I had a mother who taught me that no matter how little you have, there is still enough to share with those who have less. I had a brother and two sisters who kept me real and on my toes (I was the eldest). I had friends who were fun and crazy, but still as loyal as a person could ever find. I had two children so I had to be more responsible and caring.

Most of my strength has come from my wife Ellen, who stood by me during all the insanity I put myself through. She put up with my addictive behavior. I learned I had choices: I could stay in a dark room and live in the past, or I could step out into the light, hold my head up, and walk to the future.

I stumbled through half of my lifetime, now others can lean on me. That is a strength I am very proud of. Jane Goodall (the primatologist) said in one of her books, "I realize I can't change the world, but I can change my part of the world and hope others are changing theirs." The homeless have become part of my world and I am part of theirs. We learn from each other.

The most important lesson I have learned is to try and always respect other people. So much of our world shows disrespect for people's cultures, religions, races, status, gender and sexual orientation. A little respect goes a long, long way.

I realize what a wealthy man I am, though I don't have much money in my pockets or in the bank. My wealth is tied to my family, my two children, my wife, my friends, the homeless included. I have a checkbook full of all the wonderful souls who volunteer, and a bank account full of souls who have stumbled and fallen from great heights but still get up, brush themselves off, and walk towards a light which might still look much like the darkness. I know where my wealth lies: in people.

———◆◆▸◀◆◆———

My wife and I have believed for years that we knew each other before this life, in another lifetime. Maybe that sparked the crazy dream I had. We were both on another planet unlike the earth. It had a sun like ours, but many moons of different colors. Our skin was grey and our eyes were yellow and narrowed. We wore no clothing: there was no shame or vanity there. It was beautiful and peaceful. We were having a conversation about how we both felt as if we had known each other in another life... the circle had continued.

The least that this story will do is bring a smile to your face as you think "Boy this guy is one crazy sunnuvabitch!" And you would be right. The best part is, nothing hurts my feelings about that. I am proud to be a crazy sunnuvabitch. Look me up sometime; I'm the old guy with the ponytail and the Harley hat near the door of the shelter, who may just be the richest man in the world. Have a good life, and try to help others to have a good life too!

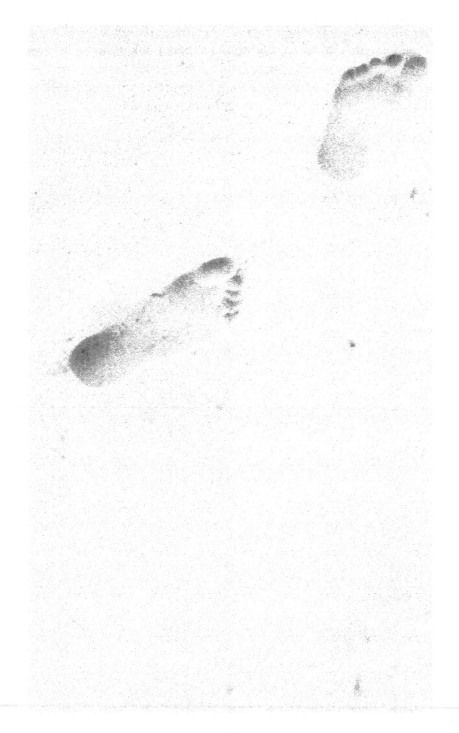

EPILOGUE
Sandbox

Man is but a speck of sand
infinitely small on the beach
hurrying, worrying, jumping at things
that seem beyond normal reach
searching for fame or glorious wealth
thinking this will ease all their pain
yet sometimes lacking the common sense
to bring themselves in from the rain
If only we could see ourselves
as innocent children today
mixing races and ideas
in the schoolyards where they play
not running blind into the night
to find what life has planned
just laughing in the sandbox
at a small handful of sand.

———◆◆✕◆◆———

The last chapter you read was meant to be the last chapter in this book. Things change, and sometimes very quickly. While trying to rewrite and organize these chapters, the world has changed immensely. COVID-19 has invaded the world, raging across our country and all the others. The homeless shelter I work in has had to close its doors.

We only have a shelter because the local churches give us a space. All the churches have closed down and are holding virtual services. Those of us who work the shelter are trying to provide transportation for our guests to state shelters which are still open.

The only good news to share is that the homeless numbers in our location have dropped immensely from past years.

We have a very young guy working as a navigator in this situation for us, social services and our local police station. He helps find housing, work, and rehabilitation spots for drugs and alcohol. There are also agencies providing support for the problems stemming from mental illness.

Here's the strange thing (as if COVID isn't strange enough): when I told my wife I would have the winter to myself and not have to work the shelter, I was excited to be able to put energy into other things. Finishing this book that I have been writing for many years, playing some music, planning next year's garden, and getting back to woodcarving, something I hope to get better at.

Instead, I find myself missing the people who help out at the shelter, and the new friends I have made. I miss our staff of volunteers who always have positive attitudes. Mostly, I miss the guests themselves. The nights I see them laugh, the times I see them share the little they do have.

This shelter has worked its way into my very heart and soul. I thought it would be a relief not to go there at night. Instead, it's like losing an old friend. Talking to the board members and other coordinators, they seem to feel the same way.

If you have never volunteered your time to any organization that works to better peoples' lives, you are missing out on a reward that is like no other. You are missing out on a larger part of the human experience. Even if you find yourself uncomfortable at first, you will get better at it, and it will grow on you. Take the step. Take a chance. Move on to a new experience and a new world beyond the one you know.

In the incredibly hard times we're living in, it's valuable to stop what you are doing once in a while, look in a mirror, and remember who you are and the things that are important to you. Don't watch the news too much: it is filled with sorrow and hopelessness. That feeling is like an angry river pulling us underwater, making us struggle to take another breath.

Find positive things to do, to read, to act upon. Remember the saying "This, too, shall pass" because it will. When you look in the mirror in the future, you will see a much stronger person. You have moved through a horrible time on our planet, and you have survived. If you have helped other people who were struggling then, there is no need to look back: you know exactly who you are now.

———◆◆◆◆———

I have written this book in the hopes of informing people more on the trials and tribulations around homelessness, and to illustrate all the similarities we have as human beings. I hope parts of it made you laugh, I hope parts brought tears to your eyes, and I hope it helped lead to greater acceptance and understanding of humans who live different lives than you do. Most of all, I hope it communicates the idea that respect may just be the most important element to human existence.

I have not written this book to make money: please share it with others you think would enjoy it.

I leave you with a quote from a very young actor and author that moved me greatly:

Karl Kristian Flores wrote "Don't tell the wealthy that the nightly humming they hear in order to sleep is made possible from distant wheels of a midnight cart being rolled by a man who dreams of a bed!"

———◆◆◆◆———

Arthur P. Palmer

Some Final Notes To Friends

- To Tree Man, a true success story. We need a lot more of them.

- To Paul, one of the kindest, most gentle souls I have ever met. His illness and torment did not stop until his heart did.

- To David, a loveable young soul, who drank himself to death.

- To Micah, a lover of the arts, as Don McClean wrote in *Vincent:* "Now I understand what you tried to say to me. How you suffered for your sanity. How you tried to set them free. They would not listen, they did not know how. Perhaps they'll listen **NOW**."

Arthur P. Palmer

For More Information on How You Can Help

NationalHomeless.org

EndHomelessness.org

Streetwise.org

HomelessLaw.org

Handup.org

CovenantHouse.org

NCHV.org

To contact the author, please email:

HumorHumilityHomelessness@gmail.com

Arthur P. Palmer

CPSIA information can be obtained
at www.ICGtesting.com
Printed in the USA
JSHW080614041122
32579JS00001B/8

9 781088 051207